Request

This is my second book after "Chitrakoot ka Itihas aur Kala-Sthapatya", which is actually a 'treasure' of the feelings that burst out of my heart at some time in my life.

I don't know how much word-power I have, but I have tried my best to put the curiosity and feelings that arose in my mind into words. I am indebted to my parents, who prepared such a fertile soil for literature at home and nurtured it with such values that literary vision and consciousness could flourish and blossom in me.

I also salute all those people, places and circumstances due to which thoughts or feelings in any form could blossom from the conscious heart, taking support from the unconscious mind.

This poetry collection "Pranay Manjusha" is actually a translated version in English of my earlier Hindi book "Meri ikyavan Kavitayen- Pranay Manjusha" This book "Pranay Manjusha" is a collection of my poems which contain within itself various aspects like affection, love, struggle, conflict, society, nation and science.

In bringing this poetry collection to perfection, my dear younger brother 'Divya Prakash Sisodia', who himself is a new writer, and my dear 'Anoop Upadhyay', who typed the words and helped in completing the work. I am sincerely thankful to both of you.

Apart from this, my wife Rachna Pathak has given as attractive cover to my life, in the same way she has selected cover page and filled colours for the cover page of this book . The attractive cover page of this book would have remained incomplete without your vision.

Finally, I thank "Rajmangal Prakashan", with whose support the publication of this poetry collection has been possible.

If any word from this book can touch the veins of the readers' hearts, it will be my good fortune. At the same time, if any words or feelings cause momentary pain to anyone, I ask for forgiveness for those words or feelings.

Date- 29/09/2025 **Dr. Sanjeev Pathak**

Index

1. Shri Guruve Namah

First of all,

There should be a

Respectful touch of feet.

And sweet contact

With a Pure heart.

You are completely healthy,

Every moment is yours.

This is our best wish.

In every birth,

We became your disciples.

At every moment,

We become your followers.

The lesson of education

That you taught.

You made it bright

Through your thoughts,

Words and actions.

And with your blessings,

Let us just keep moving forward.

By working hard like Eklavya,

Reaching the same height as Dhruva

2. Morning beauty

The natural moments of nature,

Seem amazing to me.

Its wonderful form is,

The embodiment of consciousness.

Nature's lovely morning is,

A delight to millions of hearts.

Every voice of the morning cuckoo is,

The gem of sweet speech.

The red colour of the eyes is,

like the red colour of the morning.

The reddish glow of the morning ,

Gives curiosity and peace to mind.

The bloody rays of the morning,

Like the virgin dream of a beautiful lady.

Please wake up,

The morning is saying.

Don't get robbed,

The beauty of morning.

Don't let the beautiful morning,

Get lost anywhere.

3. My Heart

My heart,

When you had to stop?

Why didn't you express it?

May be,

I would have sorted myself,

Some how way by then.

Perhaps,

I would have found the treasure of the name "Ram",

In every moment of my life.

Perhaps or else

I would have laid myself down

In each of her paths.

My heart,

When you had to bow down ,

Why didn't you express it?

May be,

I would have made "enemy "

Bigger than myself.

Perhaps,

I would have made his subservience

Reside in every moment of my life.

May be or myself,

I would have fallen at their feet.

My dear heart,

Whenever you want to stay,

Please express it!

I would give happiness to some one.

And take happiness from others.

4. Perhaps, blurred image is my love

Today again,

I was searching for relief in solitude,

The same sadness, the same silence, and the same restlessness.

And a blurred image of you.

I was far away,

But I longed to be with you.

Apparently,

'Getting you' was just a dream for me,

But in that very dream,

I was finding my victory.

Although I knew that,

I was losing,

I could hear the sound of defeated footsteps every moment.

But even after losing,

I could not break down.

Because I love my beloved,

And the synonym of love is only creation,

Then how could I break down?

We couldn't get the right ,

To steal 'you' from you.

But yes,

We had to create love,

In our imaginations.

So stealing you from your shadow,

And living with a blurred image,

May be ,this is my love.

5. If only I had my own dream

When I was sleeping at night,

And somewhere,

I was lost in a dream.

The embodiment of beauty was in front of me.

Yet, I keep wondering again and again,

Who was she?

As soon as I started solving many questions,

The answers also supported me quite well.

The question was,

Where is she from?

The answer came,

It was the morning bud of the garden of beauty.

When I thought,

Who was she?

The answer has come now,

It is your's.

What do I do now?

I myself am afraid of such happiness.

When the question came to me,

Where to go?

So while my question remained short,

The answer became detailed.

Right now it is your wish,

But tomorrow,

It will be your life.

Only when she becomes mine,

I will truly know her.

Then I woke up,

And realized that

It was all a dream.

Looking up again and again,

This is all I think about.

I wish,

Could This dream just become true!

6. Love

What will i do ?

By taking donations like alms?

What will I do in return of love?

If you don't love me with all your heart.

With empty respect,

What will I do?

When did I say?

Keep me close to your heart.

You should always remain in my mind.

Remembering you,

What will I do?

When I don't meet you,

So what will I do by staying awake all night?

When you did't come,

What will I say to my heart?

What to say to the mind?

Neither will I become a poet,

Nor will I write poetry.

7. Terrorized Kashmir

Today, even in Kashmir,

Hatred is strong.

If you look carefully now,

This atmosphere is everywhere.

Everyone is ready to fight today.

The sword 'drenched in blood' is in every hand today.

Cities are being burnt for light.

Death is being distributed for the sake of life.

Today the vermilion of foreheads,

Were destroyed by the terrorism.

Whiteness appeared on the red veil of the brides.

To eradicate this darkness of hatred.

Who get lost on the path

To get them on the right path,

O God! Listen to my prayer,

Please Send again any Chishty or Nanak.

There should be brotherhood,

Between humans,

This is our message.

Only this is our message.

8. Friend's Songs

Those songs have come out from my heart today,

The One an old friend of mine used to sing.

That song was melodious, full of sweetness.

Despite being new,

It was inclined towards the old.

Every word of the song was a symbol of skill.

Every canto of the song was indicative of the ancient.

I will hardly ever be able to forget that song of friend.

I can hardly hold back my tears,

When I remember her?

I will always remember my friend's songs.

Whenever I remember her feelings,

Will keep making me cry.

The nectar of 'Geetamrit' was touched in friend's song.

Later it was known that Friend had 'a pot of honey' on his lips.

Those songs will keep on affecting my heart,

For as long as possible,

From my mouth until then,

Those songs will continue to be sung.

9. Kashmir

Today, I am taking a picture of Kashmir.

Today, I consider that heaven to be hell.

Once Noor-Jahan had called it heaven.

But in today's Kashmir, pain is immersed.

Whenever the pain of losing' loved ones' arises?

The heart beats keep stopping and then increasing.

Today I look at Kashmiri's picture.

Instead of a beautiful scene, I see a pile of blood.

Once upon a time,

Kashmir used to be a union of two hearts.

Now who looks at Kashmir?

Today I roam around in the gardens of Kashmir.

Instead of juicy fruits,

I see bloody pieces.

Today I see the picture of Kashmir.

Now I again consider heaven as hell.

O Lord! Do something ,

So that Kashmir becomes heaven again.

10. The pursuit of beauty

This intoxication of the eyes,

Is a symbol of madness.

This virgin moisture of your rosy petal lips,

Is the dream of the nights of lovers.

This pinkness of the cheeks,

Is a symbol of perfection.

Skill in emotion and expression,

Is the pleasure of love.

The soft words coming out of the mouth ,

Are giving continuous respite to love.

The presence of the Bindu on the forehead ,

Is the identity of Indian culture.

Flying hairs are kissing your eyes and forehead ,

This whole thing looks so beautiful.

Such a beautiful girl like this,

Would be the core of my heart.

I am trying to make your

difficulties my own.

I don't know how true I am?

You are my belief in every truth.

11. Heart or mind

My mind has gone crazy

With her memories.

Along with madness,

The mind also became alien.

The heart also became a legend,

In this game of fun.

The mind tried to convince the heart,

But the heart went crazy.

Whenever I remembered her,

The mind wandered over the heart.

In the desire of fun,

The heart is lost in her imaginations.

Seeing what happened next,

The mind felt sorry for itself.

What had to happen,

Has happened.

The heart reached

At the point of fun.

My mind was also tempted.

I became a moth of her picture.

12. More beautiful than I imagined

More beautiful than I imagined,

How beautiful are you?

Even when you come in my dreams,

You are far away from me.

I still remember

The beautiful gaze of those eyes.

The radiance of that face

Is an exception even for Rati.

More beautiful than I imagined,

How beautiful are you?

Even when you come in my dreams,

You are far away from me.

That day we meet on the path ,

And then stop by again.

I still remember ,

Not being able to take even a step on the path.

More beautiful than I imagined,

How beautiful are you?

Even in my dreams,

You are away from me.

The pink glow of those lips

Is still lingering in my eyes.

The ecstatic speed of those legs

Is an exception, even for a deer.

More beautiful than I imagined,

How beautiful are you?

Even in my dreams,

you are far away from me.

My eyes are eagerly waiting

To see that face.

If we cannot see,

Then everything is worthless for these eyes.

You are more beautiful than I imagined,

How beautiful are you?

Even in my dreams,

You are far away from me.

The pinkness of those cheeks

Puts even roses to shame.

Become imaginary,

Of my imagination.

This is , the only wait.

You are so beautiful,

Beyond my imagination.

You come in my dreams,

But you are still far away from me.

13. Desire for the dust

A youth is naive

In his childhood.

Due to this foolishness

He troubles everyone.

When he gets a little older,

He is scared of going to school,

His family members scold him

And send him to school,

After saying ' no' he has to say 'yes' for school.

Eventually becomes trapped,

In the school's siege.

It takes some time to get a foothold,

But gradually it gets established.

First he learns Ka, Kha, Ga, Gha

And later adopts the word.

Strengthened by the essence of words,

A sentence is also formed.

When he becomes strong,

With the weapons of words.

Then you have to fight,

A battle of High school and Intermediate.

Even after good results,

Youth still have desires.

I may get a good percentage,

Be it honours or merit,

Or, I may find some other way.

Then we get the result,

We get a name like Art, Science or Commerce.

This is where the car stops,

And the young man's talent is passing,

Through deep hard work.

Ultimately only the shine remains;

Who ever deserved what?

Got the same path.

The story has not ended yet,

Another desire has begun.

Now I want Bride then son or daughter again.

This sequence will continue.

In the end,

The only desire is for beautiful death

As garland of clay .

14. Sensation of the heart

A beautiful girl came like lightning,

I felt very happy.

When she passed in front of me ,

My heart ached after seeing her.

Then mind also showed its magic,

Mind desired to become shadow of that girl.

My heart wanted to describing that girl,

My eyes also wanted to see that beautiful face.

Seeing the tricks of the mind,heart and eyes,

Without thinking about the future.

The body set out on its own.

The body followed that beauty in her desire,

The speed of the body was fast,

But there was hesitation.

It was nothing,

It was only just a sensation of heart.

15. In the blink of an eye

Whenever I saw you,

Something happened inside me.

It was a strange sight,

Beautiful girl was standing in front of my eyes.

Now what next?

In the game of eyes,

The scene became worth seeing.

The same thing comes up again and again,

It has become a support for the future.

Whenever I met that beautiful lady,

My eyes automatically stop.

It is not my fault in this,

And not her fault either.

When eyes meet and stop,

The perspective becomes something like this.

16. Attraction

I love her very much,

I consider her supreme among all.

This is not my imagination,

But my inclination.

It is not my imagination

But the pull of my beloved's attraction.

Dreamy dreams also came

And my eyes also connected their eyes.

Before the train reached the station,

There was some speculation.

I reached close to her,

There was still some distance,

Then why did I stop?

There was one reason for my staying here,

And that was because she was shy.

Despite everything,

The voice betrayed me.

Voice was also feeling shy.

I reached the target,

Because the target also stopped.

I am not the one to reach,

But, I was inclined to do so.

There was no other aim,

This was only Just pull of the beloved's attraction.

17. A Destructive View of Love

A big hearted people are such that,

They come through the door and go through the windows.

Because the world doesn't let you come in first.

Once you come in,

It doesn't let you go.

When has the world been obsessed with love?

That is why Laila-Majnu and Heer-Ranjha have been great.

For love,

The role of rebellion against society,

Has been played by a lot of people.

It seems a bit strange to me

That lovers write blood letters with their blood.

The pull of love is definitely there,

But it feels a bit foolish.

The reason for lovers Running away from home,

It's due to become more crazy in her memories.

Have you ever thought?

Those who will run away from home.

Hardly anywhere else,

Will be able to succeed.

Because those who will not live in own house,

Will they be able to shine at all in this cluster of houses (world)?

Those who embrace poison,

He used to be stupid,

Because by swearing on love,

They just kill their love.

My request to those idiots,

Who take the help of love, and tarnish it.

For new lovers,

Various types of arts are allocated.

Grow in love,

Move forward with love.

Because the tendency of love is 'constructive'

Not 'destructive'.

18. You became a target

Whenever I remembered you ?

I hurt myself.

Like a crazy man,

Wandered into the world.

In those beautiful moments,

Everything kept forgetting.

Every moment I kept tormenting myself,

With those memories.

Continued diving in the contemporary era.

Seeing your picture,

My imagination kept running.

I kept making 'every moment of yours' mine.

I continued making 'that path of yours' my path.

Abandoning my own goal,

I kept 'making you' my goal.

Sometimes you

And sometimes I am in this illusion,

I kept forgetting myself.

Trapped in the trap,

Which I created for you.

I kept turning this game of life,

Into a gambling ground.

I kept decorating myself,

In the rows of crazy people.

19. You and only you

Seeing your gait,

The deer in the forest are tempted.

Seeing your beauty,

Even the moon gets scared.

After getting your coolness,

Even the sandalwood tree would melt.

After listening to your voice.

Even the cuckoo becomes dumb,

Seeing your beauty,

Even 'Rati' would bow down.

Seeing your radiance,

Every shine becomes pale.

Looking at your eyes,

I feel like settling in them.

What should I say after seeing you,

Even words are falling short now.

20. Lonely-love

The one whom,

I attracted with all my heart,

In whose memory

I lost myself.

My heart is crying,

To become The pillar of that heart .

And to unite that heart with itself.

Yet, any how?

I explained it to you.

The voices were mute,

But the eyes spoke.

I was not aware of her agony,

but I increased my own agony.

I would see her on the way,

My neck would turn automatically

To getting a glimpse of love.

We met for a short time,

But I captured her image,

In every moment.

I was not aware of her desire,

But I increased my own desire.

True lovers definitely know

About their love.

Even after knowing this,

I kept myself away from reactions.

The true expression of love is through the eyes.

I also got that hint from her eyes,

Then why myself

Trapped with questions?

There are many moments in life.

I am grateful for those moments,

That bring me closer to you.

21. As often happened

I thought,

May be it might be the same there too,

As has often happened.

The agony of one has today,

Wreaked havoc on the other.

I thought may be I was confused,

As has often happened.

.

My heart is worried about,

Whether she will speak or not.

I thought

I would definitely say those three words,

As has often happened.

No matter,

How she feel ?

Without thinking about it,

Every lover has done his duty.

When A crazy boy pursued too much,

She definitely spoke,

As has often happened.

I want to meet,

But can't speak.

After Struggling,

Gradually we are able to move forward.

As has often happened.

22. I saw you at the party yesterday

Like I saw you,

In function yesterday.

Just like that,

You came in my thoughts at night.

I was not able to sleep,

Even though I wanted to sleep.

Every moment related to you,

Was tormenting me.

Sometimes bringing the bride,

On the stage (Mandap)with you.

Sometimesyou laughfacing back,

At the stage(Mandap).

Just this,

Over and over again, was tempting me.

In between,

Getting a slight glimpse of you.

I was decorating,

That long moments with you.

I thought maybe,

Today, I will say something.

But what is this?

When you came in front of me,

I was scared to even look at you,

Your arrival with the bride at the wedding venue,

Filling the hearts with romance.

It felt good that people were noticing my desire,.

I felt bad, because people were staring at her beauty.

It felt good that people were calling him by my name,

My friends also started calling my name loudly after seeing her.

I thought, I won't have to bear the distance today.

Again and again I become yours,

And then I become a stranger.

Why it is so ?

A gaze of yearning,

Wanted to say something again and again.

You were coming for taking food,

Just like a bird.

Flying again and again with straws,

Your food was something like this.

I was trying again and again to understand this act.

But why ?

Whereas you were not a bird.

Perhaps because of you,

I could not see the hero of that mandap, the 'groom'.

Because my eyes were busy again and again,

In searching for my beloved.

Taking the chenna (sweet dish) in the mouth,

And eating it like this.

Puffing up your cheeks,

And showing me side of beautiful face.

What should I understand by this?

Is this love or burning my heart.

That night I could not sleep even for a moment.

Everything was lost in those moments in your memories.

Once, while I was lying down,

A few drops fell on my eyelids.

Why so ?

I keep thinking,

Is this love?

23. Love Later

I wrote a love letter,

And was looking postmaster.

I was feeling very distressed,

My heart was burning like a graveyard.

The memories were coming morning and evening,

That was completing the letter.

I did not know how to complete a letter?

But I loved being her lover only.

I was thinking that,

The snake should die.

And the stick should not break.

There should be love,

And there should be no wrinkles in relationships.

The more delay in sending the letter,

The more so pain felt in my heart.

The new words gradually,

kept coming,

And brought life for the heart.

Today my sorrows have ended.

Beacuse of "spring of my letter" has arrived.

24. Momentary wave of joy

I will celebrate,

thought of meeting you.

She did not open her mouth,

she did not look at me for a moment.

No matter how,

After much suffering?

The day was spent in happiness.

The wave of happiness seemed to have disappeared.

I thought,

You would be happy.

Because emotions pulled me in, again.

When nothing happened,

The horse of imagination started running.

You are in front,

Both of us are chirping.

Some other people are also watching us.

When will the horse of imagination stop?

No one knows.

Night passed,

Then the same feelings won.

25. The past moments... How do I forget them?

Today I realized a new thing,

Till now I was a huge failure.

What hope was cherishing?

In which fantasies,

I was getting lost?

This new feeling troubled me a lot,

And made me cry a lot.

Why was I feeling

The same old things?

I knew that,

This dreamlike feeling was going to leave me now.

Perhaps that is why,

The flow of tears was moving in a disciplined manner.

I wanted to get lost in those moments.

Perhaps that past moment, was so deeply attached to me,

So that I could not hear the new song of the future.

I could not prepare myself along with my new friend.

Was my motivation weak?

Or my deep faith in 'my own inspiration' was weak?

Be anything ,

My inspiration may be lacking,

Or my faith may be cracked.

May be,

Our all above weakness are true.

Of which I was unaware till now.

I just gained new awareness,

Old feelings, old songs, and old friends.

Cannot be preserved for life.

26. Expression versus social constraints

Perhaps our love did not have the passion to fill you with yearning.

Maybe there was no attraction in our eyes,

That can keep your eyes fixed on us.

Perhaps our speech did not have the sweetness

That could stop your steps for a moment.

May be our personality did not have that tenacity,

That can bring you closer to us.

Perhaps that radiance was not in our form,

Who can groom you for us.

Maybe our heart is miserly,

Who could not deal with your heart.

Or maybe there is some compulsion of the heart which I could not express to you.

My love is only for you,

I could not say just this.

But how does he say?

Who could not even see the faith in love towards him.

We needed your trust in our expression.

But what do we do?

You kept faith under the veil of shame.

Yet we stand firm that it is not your fault.

This is how trust is shaken under social pressure.

I could not muster the confidence to express it.

I definitely got inspiration to understand social constraints.

27. Yes, the dying flame has remembered

Yes, I have loved truly,

Although I have seen you in hiding.

When I was close,

I falsely denied it.

When I went away,

I remembered you every moment.

Yes, I have fallen in true love.

I have tried to get you ,

In front of me.

I have had a conversation with myself,

About the grief of going away.

You were happy with yourself,

But I remembered you in every happiness.

I have recited so many ghazals for you.

You don't know,

But yes, I have loved truly.

Well,only to you,

I just accepted you as mine, after losing to destiny,

I forgot you,

But I was able to preserve your feelings.

Yes, I have truly loved.

I have just loved truly.

The 'dying flame' has lit up the burning flame.

In that light,

I remembered her for the last time.

What to say now?

What to listen to now?

Yes, I have fallen in true love.

28. I will turn into stone

Now even 'seeing her' has just become a memory.

Now even my love has become just a complaint.

Well, I have felt them a lot.

If remembering any one person is a crime.

So it is true,

I have committed this crime again and again.

The truth is,

Every moment of mine belongs to her.

Then why do we have to steal 'their memories' from the society?

Whenever we thought

We thought of her only.

Whenever we looked,

We saw her only.

Then when every moment of mine is her ,

So what kind of guard is this society?

Even if I don't meet you,

I will still live.

There is a little attraction,

Perhaps it is one-sided.

Still, anyhow?

I will live.

I never thought that,

One day I would pass through such a path.

I will see you on the path,

I will extend my last hand to reach you.

I extend my hands with the hope that you will come back to that path again.

In the above hope,

I will turn in to stone.

29. This Society and Me

Why after all?

Your feeling,

Does n't let me sleep.

There is a moment,

When I feel you away from me?

And I start thinking about you.

When I get tired of thinking,

Then I find you close to me.

Till yesterday,

You were my inspiration.

But maybe today,

You are my weakness.

I forgot my destination.

In my love for you,

I forgot to move with the speed of time.

How can I be persistent and reach my goal?

To be strong one needs perseverance.

Where can I find that determination?

Only then in the future,

there won't be that order.

Which I felt till yesterday.

I know,

I am a little wrong.

Whereas this society is completely wrong.

These Respected people areasking me,

To improve myself.

Because they know that,

This conservative society which can never improve.

So see, I have improved myself,

by flowing in the flow of society,

Today I have become completely wrong.

30. Creation

You are a creation created for me,

You are also a beautiful experience.

Traveling with you,

Wherever you are now.

Ever since,

You came into my life.

The garden of heart became happy,

And auspicious from then on.

Two buds appeared in the garden,

These buds are not just parts of the plants.

Irrigation is the most beautiful conservation of soil, roots, stem and water flow.

Clouds of joy and love gathered.

The buds will break one day,

And will fall off from the plants one day.

This feeling kept coming in my mind just like that.

Even in spring,

This feelings kept making the plants cry.

The acts of creation are sweet dreams.

Creation and destruction are the ornaments of time.

I will come one day,

Then you will feel shy.

Listen to my echoes and teach me,

The lessons of music and dance.

32. An Unwanted Destination

We too sometimes,

In the middle of the river,

Flowed with strong currents.

Thought that,

We will flow fast.

With the water stream,

Will neverleave.

With time,

from time,

Will reach the target.

But I did not know,

When did the water flow leave ?

How did the dream gradually break?

And what about us,

We were blocked by weeds.

Long before the target,

Caught on the edges.

33. Fog

The sound of the cloud's on ground,

Was really heard,

Or that it was just my illusion.

Is the weather becoming romantic,

Or has the fog deceived my heart?

Sometimes,

deception also becomes necessary,

In the Mahabharata,

deceit became

A basis of the war.

Whatever it is,

Now the white clouds look like Indralok.

And that girl wrapped in a kaftan,

Looks like an angel in the clouds.

It's all a result of

one's perspective towards the scene.

34. Father

Whenever I felt it,

I saw my father's image.

In every difficulty,

Received invisible blessings.

Even in the absence of father ,

We have to embellish our father's feelings.

Even in slippery conditions,

The finger has to be kept firmly on the ground.

I wish to God,

Just this much.

May some rays of 'Surya', who is like a father,

Fall on us every moment.

35. Good luck!

May your heart be always ,

Filled with fragrant flowers.

Youth is like spring,

The morning is joyful.

Let new lamps of hope

Be lit in life.

May your life be filled with love,

And your mind be filled with sharpness.

May you always touch new heights ,

May everything of yours be auspicious !

36. My Daughter

My courtyard is filled with the songs 'Run Jhun- Run Jhun'.

While walking on knees, anklets ringing softly.

When my daughter speaks with stammering words.

My heart also becomes filled with joy.

When my daughter hugged me as soon as she said Papa-Papa.

I will become Rana's Chetak and then my daughter will ride it.

Clinging to the mud,

My little one keeps crying with big tears.

If ever her mother fights with me,

My daughter scolds me a lot.

My daughter gives a lot of happiness with her sweet words.

37. ISRO-A Great Salute

Today Pragyan is going,

To meet the Moon.

ISRO has given it again,

India has got new honour.

This is a new beginning,

Joined as global power.

Now, Pioneering ISRO is,

The new world leader in space.

Respected ISRO,

Ambitious ISRO,

I salute your incredible struggle and success.

38. End of terror

As in the past four wars,
Why does recurrence happen?

The enemy should not consider,
India's tolerance as weakness

Until how long,
Will such terrorist acts take place?

Message of The Pahalgam,
Send it via Brahmos.
Take down all the missiles and cannons,
On Pakistan's chest.

Fond of Pak's terrorizing again and again,
Complete it once.
This is my appeal to you,
Respected 'Government of India'.

39. Imagine-what would the literary world be like?

Surdas would have woken up,

Kabir would have read,

Tulsi would have been a fool,

Think about it ,

What would the literary world be like?

There would have been no drinking of affection,

There would have been no mother's love.

Neither there would be Radha-Krishna Raas (love)

Nor there would be Phaag(Holi) in Barsana.

There would not have been a strong attack on Hindu-Muslim traditions.

Neither there would have been embellishment of literature

Nor there would have been humanistic incarnation of 'Shri Ram'.

40. Unanswered Questions

Why did 'Yogmaya' appear,

To protect the incarnation of Krishna?

Why Did The birth of Shaktirupa 'Yogamaya' also,

Happen with Krishna Murari birth only?

Why Did bet happen?

Only on the daughter,

To safe Son,

In love of Son.

Why was 'Yogmaya' opposed to protect the incarnation of Krishna?

Why was the drama of 'transfer of incarnate souls' enacted in Mathura-Vrindavan?

'Yogmaya' was the form of Shakti.

Krishna was also an incarnation.

Why was the bet placed on the 'female'incarnation

To protect the 'male' incarnation?

The papers of the old book,

Are getting scattered now.

How will you collect,

Yourself now?

41. Heart begins to beat with you

Ever since you came

In front of my eyes.

You are getting included

In every page of my life.

Even if unintentionally,

You are making fragrance in every moment of mine.

Now I have to probe myself.

Wait a bit ,

I have to tell my heart again and again.

I used to think that,

My heart is "lifeless".

It is dead,

but, seeing you

It wants to talk to you.

42. Old Pages

As if old pages started appearing before me.

A strange curiosity,

Just to get lost in the past.

That Cluster of mango's flower(manjri)

That Fighting with your loved ones.

That water-bearer girl at the well

That swaying of the mustard tree in field

We say that we have left everyone behind

And have come far ahead.

We are proud of ourselves

That we have achieved development.

In this journey of development,

We became slaves of ambitions.

Even the cheerful faces have now become sad.

We left a lot behind,

And say, we brought development.

43. Little Angel

Like a delicate bud of nature,

This little laughter is a new arrival.

The lips would open slowly and she would fall asleep,

A suppressed laughing would spread behind the closed lips.

When she cries,

It becomes bitter.

She would melt the mother's heart with her loud cries.

Seeing this scene,

Standing at a distance,

I keep thinking about this again and again.

How could the whole world reside in such a tiny life?

44. Read and do something

When the Sun would rise in the house,

Before actual Sunrise.

The tap turns on,

The bucket clinks,

The Water falls ,

And we children would wake up.

After getting up in morning

We all start studying.

While we were studying,

'Queen sleep' comes

And put us to sleep

Then father comes,

Wakes up us

And say, 'carefully Study and do something'

This is in your best interest.

But still we think about who created this 'devil study'.

Ultimately after studying

We got to shore.

Oh Lord!

This is my only prayer that,

May the rays of the same 'fatherly Sun' be upon us

A little in every moment.

45. May the winds of welfare blow for all

Let the lamp burn,

New love blossom.

Let reverence and sacred feelings awaken in the hearts.

With the blessings of the seniors,

The juniors should also receive affectionate love.

May a wind of welfare blow

From 'God's blessings' for all.

46. Diana - Divorce from Life

Today I present,

The Diana-Charles Chronicles.

Somewhere there was love,

As well as somewhere there was conflict.

This was a tragic romance.

On July Nineteen Sixty One, Diana's rays of destiny(birth) spread across the world.

Charles, a twelve-year-old , was wandering for understanding the world.

Charles' wanderings came to an end.

When he encountered by beautiful eyes of sixteen-year-old girl Diana.

Both continued to meet at polo game.

The matter kept on increasing.

And the fire of love started turning into the fire of marriage.

After three years of difficult separation,

The separation became a happy ending for the couple.

Today, nineteen year old Diana became Charles's wife.

How would she know that this marriage will destroy her in the future.

On July twenty nine nineteen hundred eighty one ,

Diana became the bride of the British throne and Charles became the Crown Prince.

This was the call for romance.

Only for one year,

She could remain an independent princess.

She earned the title of "Mother"

After giving birth two princes William and Harry.

The Charles-Camilla Parker love story first came to light,

Through Andrew Martin's book, "Diana Her True Stories."

Once again in history,

The male race went astray first.

After that, both sides got addicted to this stray thing.

Diana was still an ideal,

And was the embodiment of charity.

Despite seeing everything,

She remained like Surdas.

It is said that

One fish makes the whole pond dirty.

A fish in the form of Charles swept away even Diana in its flood.

In August nineteen hundred ninty two,

Diana's endurance broke.

She rejected Charles and made another his power

In October nineteen hundred ninty four

From the Anna Pastern book's "Princess in Love",

The world had to endure a big kick,

Because Diana's new hook became James Hebit now

For how long could this matter be kept hidden?

James Hebit was Diana's new acceptance.

Diana's bitter conflict with Charles continued.

Age from twenty three to thirty five,

There was a pointed saw for Diana.

After the struggles,

The struggles were suppressed.

Now Diana and Charles's had their own separate garden.

Trust was lost,

And Divorce was on the horizon.

That ray of destiny was restless again today.

But in social welfare, she was completely successful.

Charles started the deviated story.

Diana unveiled the same, over and over again.

Now Diana had the power Dodi al-Fahd.

Own people of Diana betrayed her,

How long will strangers helped her ?

Diana-Fahadh were roaming around in the Mercedes.

The sharp eyes of time were staring at them.

The Mercedes was racing.

The messengers of death of the press behind her,

And ahead is the ambassador of time.

Where would Diana go?

She find death everywhere.

What did she know?

Moments later,

She would become prey.

Leaving William and Harry,

She will become the Pole Star.

Today that initial ray(Diana) has been completely engulfed by time.

There was such a thunderbolt upon the world,

As if a volcanic eruption had occurred.

Charles could not make Diana as an ideal wife

The new news on BBC was 'Diana-Divorce from Life'.

Diana will remain a good role model for social wellfare,

For ages to come.

Her Love and sacrifice as identity will become the pride of the world.

47. Meeting of the eyes

Usually things happen through eyes only,

Beautiful eyes often come into conflict with oneself.

In the battle of eyes,

Even the greatest giants bow down.

Who knows ?

How many Prithvirajes get destroyed ,

By the arrows of Sanyogita's eyes.

There are many types eyes.

Some are effective,

Some are ineffective,

Some eyes make their own.

Ineffective vision get lost in the abyss of the past,

While Effective vision become permanent in the future ,

Such as beautiful birds get trapped in the cages of eyes.

48. I have heard about my beloved

I have heard about my beloved that,

My beloved has so thin waist?

Who knows where she ties her Ghangharia?

I have heard about my beloved that there is no wave in the walking

I don't know ,

How She leaves everyone behind?

I have heard about my beloved that,

My beloved doesn't chirp at all.

I don't even know

How the cuckoo feels shy in front her?

I have heard about my beloved that,

My beloved has no appearance.

But why Even Rati also looks pale in front her.

I have heard about my beloved that,

My beloved doesn't have any garden.

Who knows where she does romance?

I have heard about my beloved that,

Not jealous in her ,

But why does she burn in the fire of love?

49. Even in defeat there was a faint victory

We remembered you.

And did it only once,

What did we know?

This will become our habit.

We did it only once,

Had talked to you.

What did we know?

I will start doing the same thing to myself.

We just for a moment,

Loved her.

What did we know?

Our every moment,

Will become a follower of that moment.

We just took a look at her,

What did we know?

It will be absorbed 'that same look' in our eyes.

We learned to move forward by taking her as inspiration.

What did we know?

The same inspiration would become my goal tomorrow.

By accepting her as our own,

We had raised some hopes.

What did we know?

That the innocent heart will start finding faith in hope.

We had only learnt how to win.

What did we know?

Only after losing her,

I will be able to cherish her.

Perhaps even in that defeat,

There was my faint victory.

Remembering that defeat,

I will find her closer to me.

50. I will hardly be able to live in separation

It seems,

That moment has come now.

We will be separated from you.

If I spend a few more moments with you,

I will hardly be able to stay away from you.

The truth is that,

Who cares about life?

The only sadness is that of separation,

Which we may not be able to see.

If we were in pain,

We wouldn't have said 'ohh'

If my life had been lost,

I would have had no complaint.

If you snatch away the one whose shadow we are,

We will remain incomplete.

After losing you,

Will create false hope of 'getting you'.

But, if we are there in that separation,

We will hardly be able to live.